Love is the Why

Diana K. McLean

WWW.TEHOMCENTER.ORG

Love is the Why
ISBN: 978-1-960326-89-8
Copyright © 2024 by Diana K. McLean

Author photo by Michael Spigarelli.

Tehom Center Publishing is a 501c3 non-profit imprint of Parson's Porch Books. Tehom Center Publishing is an imprint publishing feminist and queer authors, with a commitment to elevate BIPOC writers. Its face and voice is Rev. Dr. Angela Yarber.

To Shay
My partner in ministry and life
My Beloved

Table of Contents

Section 3: Social Justice

We live in a world that often discourages curiosity and dismisses the redeeming power of love. *Love is the Why* is a beautiful subversive invitation to dive into our wonders and explore our own whys. Diana K. McLean gently guides the reader in exploring why and also how to love ourselves, our bodies, the divine, and justice for all creation. *Love is the Why* and it is a gift to embrace and share with others.

- Rebecca Wilson, Poet & Storyteller at 10 Camels. Author of *Unraveling: Coming Out and Back Together.*

In her first book of poetry, *Love is the Why*, Diana McLean, claims herself to be a "Minister …reclaiming poet and will work to earn activist" yet her activism and poetry radiate on each page and poem with raw emotion and a call to the action of Love. As we, and she, enters middle age, she calls us to Love our bodies while allowing the guilt of the past to soften rather than simply forcing it away. We are the Divine Feminine and McLean's realization of this in her words strikes deep into each of us as we feel her words calling us to Love each body part, each archetype, each finger and wrinkle and stretch mark. Using this Love of self to become the activist, McLean further calls us to Love all those whose lives we can help and heal; from the immigrant child to the ones lost to a needless, unending war, to the very Earth Herself.

- Kelly Christine, MFA

The poems in this book are more than pieces to observe; they are our poems, written not just from McLean's heart but from our own. She reveals the real, lived humanity in all of us - from our concerns around aging, our understanding of what it means to be love and be loved, and the ways we are called to love and compassion. McLean bridges the gap between personal and universal, and heals us all with her lyrical offerings.

- Rev. Kimberley Debus, Community Minister of the Arts and Worship

Love is the Why is more than a book of poetry—it's an accessible and inclusive work that beautifully explores themes of self-love, the body, and love for others, in all forms. It resonates deeply with the essence of love in all its forms.

- J.A. Kazimer, author of *Curses! A F***ed-Up Fairytale*

Rev. Diana McLean's debut offering of reflective poems, *Love is the Why*, encourages us to contemplate our own bodies, our own connection to the divine of our understanding, and our own commitment to justice. She models vulnerability, being the love she seeks in the world. Have your journal open as you explore these poetic meditations. Pay attention to what resonates. Write in the margins what you would change in order to make it true to your own experience. Connect with what is rising in you from the verses. I literally cut out the last poem and posted it where I will see it during my morning prayers.

- Rev. Tandi Rogers, Director and Designer of the Spiritual Direction program at Meadville Lombard Theological School's Leadership Institute for Growth, Healing, and Transformation

Reclaiming activism as a mode of care, Diana's poetry is an intimate journey toward embodying love for self, for the holy, and for the world; and connects the power of the divine feminine with ordinary lives. Like Adrienne Rich and Judy Grahn, Diana M inspires and uplifts. This book is invaluable for anyone seeking profound truth and empowerment.

- Rev.Amy Beltaine, Chair, Spiritual Direction Program, Cherry Hill Seminary

Diana McLean's *Love is the Why* is rueful, grace-filled, passionate, funny, and deeply honest. In the opening section, she speaks to us of the fragility and strength of our bodies, and all the ways they connect us to our ancestors. Then, her words explode off the page as she channels the searing power of the divine feminine and releases a fierce compassion for the countless souls harmed by violence and injustice. "Women," she tells us, "write your own biographies"—and in this brilliant collection, she has done just that.

- Rev. Laura Horton-Ludwig, Spiritual Director, Life Coach, and Shamanic Practitioner

Compassion, interconnectedness, and the transformative power of poetry and ministry form the sacred geometry of *Love is the Why*. Inspiring us to act as "love's agents," McLean illuminates the infinite facets of love—desire, rage, faith, grief, wonder, and more. Through her poems, we come to understand love as home, as altar, as birthright and legacy, and as abundantly available even in the most challenging times.

- Lisa Birman, author of *How to Walk Away*

Acknowledgments

This project has been incubating for a very long time, in many forms over the years. It was certainly at least an idea by the time I finished my Master of Fine Arts in Creative Writing at Naropa University in December 2009. I am so grateful to all of my teachers there, especially Lisa Birman (whose many roles included Thesis Advisor Extraordinaire), Max Regan (who has continued to teach me in recent years, thanks to his excellent online workshops), and Selah Saterstrom, whose individual conference with me at the Summer Writing Program in 2009 resulted in a list of about ten manuscript ideas, one of which ("This Body") eventually became one of the sections of this book.

I am also grateful to every teacher, from elementary school through multiple college degrees, who encouraged me to write.

Many of my Unitarian Universalist colleagues in ministry have encouraged me to keep my writing at the center of my sense of call, knowing it to be not a hobby but a core part of my ministry in the world. Special thanks to colleague, role model, and Literary Minister Rev. Karen Hering for modeling what that can look like.

I have deep admiration and gratitude for Rev. Dr. Angela Yarber, who has ministered to the world in many ways, most recently as the founder of Tehom Center Publishing. Her commitment to publishing those who are marginalized in the mainstream publishing industry is deep and unwavering, and her support of the authors who publish with Tehom Center Publishing is robust. Without her, this book would still be an idea.

Through it all, my family has been a steady source of support and encouragement. My Dad, Jon McLean, may have told me (correctly) as a child that I wouldn't make a living as a poet, but he was proud every time I ever published anything. I wish he were here to see this book become reality. My Mom, Kathy McLean, once responded to someone saying I had very strong emotions, "Well, if she didn't, she wouldn't be a very good poet, now would she?" She continues to support and encourage me in countless ways.

My son, Aidan McLean, who is now a young adult, graciously allowed me to write about his childhood for years in a newspaper parenting column. He has equally graciously allowed me to include a few poems written to him in this book, though I imagine he may be rolling his eyes about it when I'm not looking. I'm so proud to be his mother, eye rolls and all.

Last but certainly never least, my beloved wife, Shay MacKay, has supported me in countless ways, including suggesting a personal writing retreat for the two of us while I worked on this manuscript, and she worked on one of her own. How lucky are we that our shared life is full of poetry?

Introduction

Love has been at the center of my personal theology for longer than I have understood what theology was.

When I was thirteen, I wrote this about love:

Love

> Love is like a flower
>> blooming until it
>>> shows its beauty to the world.

> Love is like a flame
>> heating us from within
>>> giving us strength
>>>> to go on.

> Love is paradise
>> peaceful, calming me
>>> after a hard day, letting
>>>> me feel special.

Clearly, I was not writing about the Valentine's Day or Hollywood type of love, but of something broader. While the wording may not be what I would use today, what thirteen-year-old me wrote about love is still part of my theology of love as our grounding, our center, our why.

At a clergy retreat in 2017, a presenter asked us "What is the song you came to sing, the song in your heart?" and my answer was "Be Love's <u>voice</u> in the world." (I had previously been saying "be Love's hands in the world.")

My discernment at that retreat was part of a years-long struggle to choose between writing and ministry, which began when I thought I had to choose between earning a Master of Fine Arts in Creative Writing and attending seminary to earn a Master of Divinity and then pursue ordination. Even after I recognized that I could do both, the early years of ministry found me not doing much writing beyond what was part of my parish ministry job: sermons, reports to the Board, newsletter columns, and so on.

In January of 2019, I wrote in a journal entry: "What would it be like to fully inhabit 'writer' and 'poet' as well as 'minister'?" In May of that same year, I wrote in another journal entry: "So here I am, back at the question of how I can reclaim a writing life (as ministry, not instead of ministry)."

Prior to working with Angela at Tehom Center Publishing, I thought that the poems that became this book were three separate themes: embodiment and body positivity; honoring the divine feminine; and social justice. Angela saw the three sections fitting together, three aspects of Love at work: self-love, love of the sacred in feminine form, and love expressed as justice (in keeping with one of my favorite quotes, "Justice is what Love looks like in public," by Cornel West). Thanks to her big-picture view, the book you are reading now came to be.

When I shared some of my journey with Angela, one story I told her was the origin of the phrase *Love is the Why* which came from a conversation in theology school and became a hashtag I used on some of my social media posts.

Here's the text from one such post I wrote on April 17, 2015 about the theology school conversation:

> I am grateful for this morning's Intro to Unitarian Universalist Religious Education class, in which Ashley Johnson kept asking "why" until she got me to say this about why we have conversations about power, privilege, and prejudice:
>
> Ashley: Why?
>
> Me: Because I want to make the world more loving, more just, more free.
>
> Ashley: Why? Breathe into it...
>
> Me: Because I love the world and the people in it. [pause] Or really, just because I love.
>
> Ashley: Who do you want to be in the world? Breathe...
>
> Me: I want to be someone who loves.
>
> And then: Ashley said what she hears underneath all that is "I *am* love."
>
> I'm not even sure I captured that completely accurately. Or that the power of it can be communicated without being in the room. But friends, it was powerful.

From there, over time, I was able to articulate that love is the "why" of my ministry–and Love-with-a-capital-L is one of the genderless names I use for the divine.

From a journal entry dated Jan 7, 2019:

Love is the Why

Why I am a minister
        and a parent
        and a partner

Why I say yes to more requests
        than might be reasonable

And why I say no
        as loudly and often as possible
        to oppression and hate

God is Love, some say.
        Maybe Love is God.

And another from Jan. 16, 2019:

Love is the Why

I <u>am</u> love.

And so are you.

Love is why we exist–life's love of life–
        and love is what calls us
            to be our best,
                most authentic selves.

Love is the Why
        behind all the best of who I am
            and how I live in the world.

Section 1: This Body

"Making peace with your body is your mighty act of revolution."
-Sonya Renee Taylor, *The Body Is Not an Apology: The Power of Radical Self-Love*

Section Introduction

I began work on this project fifteen years ago. It has taken on new shape and meaning now, in my early 50s.

It began as a set of poems, mini love letters to different parts of my body: often celebrating them, but also sometimes reclaiming them from something either I or society had labeled as "wrong" or "unattractive" (as we are wont to do with others' bodies, especially the bodies of women, trans people, and others with marginalized identities).

In the years since then, despite my own challenges with my body, I've come to have a different perspective on it in several ways.

First, I am much more aware of the privilege I carry in our society just because of the color of my skin (the pale shades we collectively call "white"). I'm also still aware of all the ways that society tries to police my body, including the overturn of Roe v. Wade and the efforts to make abortion illegal nationwide.

Second, I am much more aware of the body-positivity movement, and have been slowly learning to love and appreciate my body for what it is and how it is at this stage of my life, rather than wishing for it to be more "ideal" in some way. As I got older, "ideal" became less about weight or shape or age than about health, which was a good first step, but my friends in the disability community have helped me to understand the inherent ableism in assuming that a "healthy" body has more worth than one with any kind of illness, disability, or other "physical limitation." That was a hard learning for me—initially, even though I certainly believe all *people* have inherent worth and dignity, I had not made the step to understanding that all bodies are sacred not in spite of their "limitations" but simply because they are our bodies. They, no less than our minds or spirits, deserve to be loved just as they are.

At fifty-three, I am inescapably a middle-aged white woman. I am also a queer person, a person with multiple chronic illnesses, a person who has carried, birthed, and nursed a baby (and whose body released another tiny life before it had a chance to become more than a beginning).

I am an empty-nester, the parent of a young adult—that baby who grew inside me has gone off to college. I am not yet a grandparent and content to keep it that way for a while—forever, if that's the choice my son makes for himself.

19

The body I live in now deals with a variety of challenges—though I am never sure how much of that to attribute to my body and how much to attribute to the ills of our larger body—both the global pandemic that began in 2020 and is still present despite our collective attempts to ignore it, or the body politic that has become terrifyingly fascist-leaning in the last decade or so, seemingly faster every year.

Partly because of my relatively new understanding of myself as a person with chronic illnesses, I have granted myself permission to be kinder, more loving, to my body. Early in the pandemic, my wife and I bought a very expensive bed (we call it our "old people" bed) with remote controls that can raise the head or foot of each half. It allows us both to sleep better, and to read in bed without back twinges. Just before the pandemic, we had also purchased a higher-quality set of living room furniture than we've ever owned—just in time to spend a whole lot of time on the couch, including many many Zoom meetings and online worship services (we're both ministers) led from the safety of our own home. We are more thoughtful about the food we eat—just recently, I re-read the book Animal, Vegetable, Miracle by Barbara Kingsolver, and am paying more attention to the quality of our food, and how local it is, in an attempt to improve not only my own health but that of the planet.

Perhaps that's one of the biggest realizations: I understand on a visceral level how my body and the body of the earth are interdependent. Without the forests that are the earth's lungs, I would be unable to breathe. When all seems hopeless, it is by feeling my bare feet on soft grass or soil or warm sand that I can most easily feel grounded. When I am anxious, being in or even near a body of water soothes me.

While this project is made up of pieces focused on certain aspects of my body, I think of those parts of my anatomy now not as separate things with no obvious relationship, but as facets of my physical experience in the world —like holding a cut gemstone to the light and turning it to see it through different facets. The light comes differently through the various planes, but the gem is always one whole.

Skin

This skin, so fair
  easily bruised
  easily freckled
  easily reddened
    by sun
    by exertion
    by embarrassment

This skin, evidence
  of years attained
    little lines around eyes and knuckles
    little white spots on hands
  of injuries survived
    scars from cat claws
      from chicken pox
      from biopsies (every mole or spot a worry now)
  of milestones achieved
    faint white ring when my wedding ring is off
    faint stretch marks where a baby grew

This skin, uniquely mine
  a tattoo around one ankle
    symbols of history
      of heritage
      of values
      of faith
      of identity

This skin, thin barrier between me
    and not-me
      more permeable than it looks
        no barrier at all.

Hands

I.

These hands
        learned to write the alphabet
                before I was three
      wrote my first autobiography
              in kindergarten
              "All About Me"
      wrote my first poem
              when I was about eight
    kept a diary
              from age ten or so
              (just like my grandma's
              collection of five year-diaries)
    taught themselves to type
              on our family's first computer
    typed college papers
              and my first poetry submissions
              on a Smith Corona word processor
                    (years later, I inherited Grandma's
                          Smith Corona manual typewriter)
    still prefer pen and ink.

II.

More fine lines every year
but they make me smile
because my hands now
look like my mom's did
when she was my age

Feet

I.

These feet
    have walked sidewalks in countless cities
        in nineteen countries
        on four continents
    have wriggled in the silky-soft
        not quite slimy
        silty bottoms of lakes
        in the Ozarks and elsewhere
    have walked the sandy beaches
        of the Oregon Coast
        the North Sea
        Normandy
        Hawai'i
        Mexico
    and the rocky shores
        of Oregon
        Maine
        Alaska
    have pedaled tricycles and bicycles
        on suburban streets
        and Atlantic City boardwalks
    have been pampered at spas
        scrubbed with sea salt
        encased in mud
        dipped in paraffin
        buffed
        moisturized
        nails polished purple
    have pressed the gas and the brake
        of a blue 1984 Ford Mustang
        a white 1990 Dodge Spirit
        a brown hand-me-down Toyota Camry, year forgotten
        a green 2006 Ford Focus
        a white 2013 Ford Escape (which was Dad's until he died)
        and countless rental cars

II.

These feet
         which so often pain me now
         if I walk even 2,000 steps a day
         once easily walked 10,000 or more

walked miles
         on the streets of childhood neighborhoods
         in cities and towns in Europe
         seeing sights
                  in Turkey, Egypt, China
         to and from school
                  my own
                  and later my son's
                           when he was little enough
                                    to want or need me
                                             by his side
         in convention center hallways
         between classes on campuses
                  in Lincoln, Boulder, Denver
         in 5K "fun runs" with friends

walked labyrinths
         (my favorite spiritual practice)

walked ocean beaches
         as waves washed over them

walked forest paths
         with no fear of uneven ground
                  until the afternoon
                           I hiked too hard a trail
                                    on a smallish mountain in Colorado
                                             and came down
                                                      bundled in a litter
                                                      belayed off trees
                                                      carried by a mountain
                                                               rescue team
                  and didn't walk again
                           for months
                                    and never with the same
                                             easy confidence.

III.

Some days I wonder
if my feet will ever not hurt again
something I once took for granted
as I walked, hiked, danced
moved through my day
without hesitation
or grimacing
or limping
or stumbling
as my ankle gives way

Smile

This smile
      a little lopsided
            just like Mom's
Reveals teeth
      chipped in my sleep at age 17
            and then sanded down
                  by a dentist who told me my choices were
                      a $400 mouth guard to wear at night
                      or false teeth at 40

Well, at 40 I still have all my own teeth
      and a mouth guard
      though sometimes I still have
            the old nightmare
                  in which my teeth suddenly crumble
                  and come apart,
                  leaving me jagged stumps
                      or bare gums

The TMJ, which was bad enough one year
      to slip the disks in my jaw
            put me on a liquid diet and muscle relaxers
            and send me to months of massage therapy
      has given me no trouble since I moved away
            after the divorce.

Eyes

These eyes
     have devoured books since before school
     have needed glasses since third grade

     have watched many pregnancy tests
          show negative
   and then when least expected
          one quickly, clearly positive

     have seen my baby on ultrasound
          months before I could see him
          in the flesh
   have watched him grow
          from newborn to infant
          from toddler to preschooler
          from big boy to teenager
          to young man
   have watched
          meteor showers
          sunsets
          sunrises
          bird murmurations
          whales breaching
          northern lights

     have had gradual small floaters
          and sudden scary big ones
              (posterior vitreous detachment)

watched my child sleep
watched my beloved sleep

watched my father die
          and my mother grieve

watched life unfold
          in all its many forms.

Three Years Old, in the Back Yard

Tall lilac hedge
mirrored in my little cotton dress
  green with purple blossoms
  and a white collar
  hemmed just above chubby, tanned knees
thick, soft purple yarn
  tied around my blonde ponytail

I press my body into the hedge
  inhale deeply
  immerse myself
     in the sweet perfume

Not yet aware
  my mother did this
    before me
  and her mother
    before her
  in other yards, in other states

The lilacs now part
  of our shared story
  a sensory key to unlock memories
    decades from now

Relativity

Frozen in time
on their wedding day in 1902
he seems to be smiling a little under his mustache.

She most clearly is not.

Maybe because of how long one had to sit still for a photograph then.
Maybe not.

I never met her
   mother of the mother of my mother
but I have her rocking chair, her garnet ring
her face.

A face so like my own
people think it's me in old-fashioned costume
in a novelty photograph.

Even I have been fooled.

Mom and I looked through the jumble of photos
in Grandma's cedar chest
saying, "Here's one of Grandpa,"
or "This is when you were about two."

I picked up this one, said, "Here's me—"
then stopped, realizing
it wasn't.

I'd seen the picture before, but even so
had a flash of recognition
of my own face.

Curve of my ear
angle of my jawline
shapes of my nose, my lips, my eyebrows
height of my forehead
and slightly off-center part in my hair.

Even the slight tilt of my head
and the look in my eyes.
It's me,
looking out at myself
from a century ago.

No color here, only sepia tones
and yet
> I imagine her eyes
>> *behind her wire-rimmed glasses*
>>> *so like my own*
> to be the same
> blue-but-sometimes-green-or-gray
> as mine
> and her hair,
> although curled within an inch of its life
> and adorned with a white bow
>> *in a way mine never would be*
> to be the same
> something-between-dark-blonde-and-light brown
> as mine.

I have pictures of her
later in life
and don't see myself in them...
perhaps because I haven't caught up with her yet.

Or perhaps this portrait
caught us at an intersection
a single point in time
where we were doubled in each other.

Perimenopause

I.

busy brain, no sleep
perimenopause plus stress
bad combination

II.

Maybe people in perimenopause
    should be excused from work
        (or any unwanted human interaction)
      to keep us from being
          too blunt
          too angry
          too powerful
      for all those other people to handle

      because we are
          all
          out
          of
          fucks

III.

Drying up in middle age:

    my skin
    my eyes
    my lips
    my caring about being "nice"
        to keep anyone else happy
    my tolerance for bullshit.

Forty-Eight

(to the tune of The Twelve Days of Christmas)

For my forty-eighth birthday
        my body gave to me

twelve memory lapses
eleven bouts of brain fog
ten hours of cramping
nine acne breakouts
eight new food cravings
seven dry skin patches
six medications
five hot flashes
four new gray hairs
three back pains
two aching joints
and a case of insomnia.

My Body at Fifty

At fifty, my body is indisputably
middle-aged.

There are fine lines around my eyes,
age spots (my mom calls them wisdom spots)
on the backs of my hands,
stretch marks across my belly,
and more ample padding than in younger years.

There are places with weakness due to old injuries;
I now understand how weather and bones interact.

There are spots that need extra care,
both from me and from medical specialists,
to keep me at my healthiest.

My life now includes
       a podiatrist
       bifocals
       hot flashes
       pill organizers

My maternal grandmother lived to be 95,
and her sisters also lived into their 90s.

I figure fifty is only about my half-way point.

Maybe time for a little intermission to stretch my legs,
reflect on the plot so far,
and look ahead to what might be coming in the next act.

Body Memories

This body holds memories

of holding very still
one small hand clenching a little toy dog
while I lay in the CAT scan machine

of the feeling of almost-flight
when I learned how to ski
without falling down

of singing in choirs
from middle school to college
and in decades of churches

of stretching to hold a growing baby
then birthing him
and nursing him

of the last time
I hugged my father
hours before he died

of the first time
I kissed the woman
who became my wife

Body Routines

This body likes to
    sleep in
    wake up slowly
    eat a good breakfast
            greek yogurt or
            oatmeal or
            granola
    work at a pace
            neither too slow
            nor too frenetic
    take a lunch break
            not work through lunch
    eat a snack midafternoon
            to get through the rest of
            the workday
    eat supper
    do yoga
    stay up reading
            but not too late

    repeat

Body Wisdom

I said out loud today
       that my job reminds me
              of my abusive past marriage
said I stayed in that eight years
       survived by the skin of my teeth
              and won't do that again.

Tonight a podcast talked about
       knowing in our bodies
              when something is in alignment
                     when it is right for us
       and you reminded me
              of my upset stomachs
              my high blood sugars
              my fatigue
              my headaches

My body knows, as it did before:
       something has to change
              or I have to go.

Chronic Illness Haiku

on a fatigue day
my brain is writing checks that
my body can't cash

Skin Biopsies

I.

Ouch

mole excision hurts
in the middle of my back
hard to keep it still

II.

suture removal
skin can move naturally
such a huge relief

III.

My back is a constellation
    of scars
        and many more freckles and moles

How many more dark spots
    will become pale circles
        or pink lines?

The scars tell a tale
    and have a moral:
        wear sunscreen.

IV.

No tan for me.
I go from white
    straight to red
    then either peel or fade
    back to white again

That is, if I forget my
    SPF 80 (or whatever)
    sunscreen.

After five skin biopsies
      (benign
      but plenty frightening
      and painful)
      I rarely forget.

V.

I'm being carved away
      one small piece at a time
            as a collage of scars
                  emerges and grows

The latest wound still fresh
      stitched shut just days ago
      still sore and itchy

The one before that
      less than a year old
      still a vivid scar
      which will fade with time
            (as does the memory)
                  but neither is ever
                        fully erased.

Biopsies/Bullying

You do it slowly
cutting away
      a little piece of me
           at a time
                then cauterizing or stitching the wound
                    as if that makes me whole

it's painful
      but manageable
           in small doses

Until the day
      when I notice
           I'm covered
              in scars.

Fatigue

A gray, rainy day
      reflects (or causes?)
           my lethargy

I don't want to do anything
      except sleep
           eat a little
                do mindless things
                    (games on my phone)

No energy for work
      for writing
           for reading
                let alone for deep conversation

So when you ask
      if I'm okay
           I just say
                "I'm tired"

and it's true
      if oversimplified

           bone-weary
           exhausted
           sleep-for-days
              tired

Body Love

I.

I love my
  feet
              toenails painted purple
              delicate bones
              blue veins through fair skin
    ankles
              right one tattooed
                      (my 37th birthday gift to myself)
              left one scarred
                      (broken ankle repaired at age 44)
    hands
              Grandma wrote on a photo of me as a newborn
              that my long fingers meant
              I'd play piano.
              They look more like Mom's every year.
    eyes
              color changing with clothes
                      and mood
    hair
              with newly-discovered curl

II.

This body—my body—
        deserves my respect
                      my care
                      my love.

It is my only body
        my only home in this lifetime.

I have wasted time
        calling it   too thin
                          too heavy
                          too short
                          too slow
                          too weak

I should have been
> loving it
> caring for it
> moving it
> feeding it
> resting it
> enjoying it

My complaints
> reinforced my reality.

My love
> can change my reality.

Sizes

This body
    has been called too small
        seventh grade
        five feet two inches
        ninety-one pounds
        (the school nurse
            talked to me about anorexia)
    has been called too big
        twenty-one
        just out of college
        sudden weight gain
        no explanation
            my doctor could find
                (years later, diagnosed with PCOS
                and it began to make sense)

At forty
    I still struggled
        to find the
        "just right"
        weight.

At fifty
    I'm learning
        to love my body
            and know it is holy
                at any size.

Strength

I.

This body
>feels tonight
>like a loose collection
>of sore muscles:
>>hips
>>thighs
>>calves
>>butt
>>shoulders

I'm not complaining.

I'm transforming
>a day at a time
>an exercise at a time
>an ache at a time.

That's how it is sometimes.

II.

This body is strong.
This body gave birth to a nine-pound, two-ounce baby.
This body is flexible.
This body does the triangle pose in yoga
>and feels powerful.
This body is changing
>gaining muscle and endurance.
This body is healthy.

Yoga

Yoga makes me feel
      strong, sleek, long-muscled, sexy

I learn I'm flexible
      trying new poses

muscles are tired
mind is invigorated
body is relaxed

You may not see it
but after yoga practice
I'm taller
      as if I have finally reached
         my goal height: 5'5"

Dysphoria

mirror shows one me
camera shows another
neither feels like me

Doctor Visit

Arthritis
      and maybe asthma
            (and an unwelcome lecture about my weight
            which will lead me to find a new doctor)

I am trying so hard
      to love my body
      instead of seeing it as
            my enemy
            (or a recalcitrant child)

but it's hard in the face of
      a new inhaler
      an ankle brace
            (and predictions of increasing pain and stiffness)
      a glucometer
            I should use periodically
                  but haven't been

What the Body is Not

This body
       is not who I am.

       It is only the home
              for the real me,
     the vehicle
           to move my soul
                 through this world

If you judge me by the body I'm in
      labeling me
           female
           short
           white
           heavy
           diabetic

You will have stated facts,
      but will never know me

Uncovered

Sometimes
      I know myself to be
      a body of light
      shining steadily—
      not this body of skin, muscles, bones

This is merely the clothing I wear
      to play my role
      in the drama of life

In the quiet dark before sleep
      I slide out of all coverings
      and acknowledge
            who I am.

Power wells up in me
      from within
            above
            below

And pours through me as light
      not blinding radiance
      but a soft glow
      which nonetheless banishes shadows.

Imagine the world
      if we could know this
            about ourselves
                  from the moment of birth.

Section 2: Honoring the Divine Feminine

"The idea of Goddess is so powerfully "other," so vividly female,
it comes like a crowbar shattering the lock patriarchy holds on divine
imagery." - Sue Monk Kidd, *The Dance of the Dissident Daughter: A Woman's
Journey from Christian Tradition to the Sacred Feminine*

Section Introduction

My first connection to the idea of the divine feminine was when I read Marion Zimmer Bradley's <u>The Mists of Avalon</u> at age 17 or 18, in my first year of college. It thrilled me to open those pages and enter a world where there were priestesses serving a goddess. Even though my childhood ministers were women, so I knew women could be religious leaders, this was something markedly different: the divine, portrayed in female form, and a whole culture of women who both served and embodied the divine feminine. (Cautionary note: after re-reading that book in adulthood, and learning more about the author, I found some of it quite problematic, so this is not a reading recommendation, only a starting point for my exploration of the divine feminine.)

A couple of years later, after reading <u>A Ring of Endless Light</u> by Madeleine L'Engle (a book which was not about the divine feminine) several poems poured out of me in rapid succession, poems that felt like they came more *through* me than *from* me. The speaker in those poems was clearly feminine, and clearly with divine powers. In one, she named herself She Who Sees. This was my first experience of understanding myself as connected to the divine feminine in a mystical way.

At a clergy retreat in 2017, we were asked to choose two cards from a table spread with various tarot and oracle cards: one for our relationship with the holy and one for the holy in relationship with a challenge we were dealing with. My first card was Moon/The High Priestess (with Jewish symbols—maybe Shekinah?) and my second was Nu Kua/Order (from the Goddess Oracle). We were then asked "Where do you find the Holy?" and my response in my journal was:

> In connection to nature (especially the night sky and bodies of water). In connection with others. In images of the divine feminine. In knowledge of myself and my beloved as embodiments of that divinity in female form. In music, especially singing with women's choir, at Winter Solstice.

The next question was "How does the holy support my ministry?" to which I wrote:

> It allows me to be centered and grounded in something deeper, older, wiser than myself. It allows me to know my place in a lineage

of wise women and a lineage of ministers in this faith [Unitarian Universalism], and calls me to carry forward the work they were part of. To know myself as priestess and prophet.

When I am connected to the holy, I am courageous and bold. I feel physically taller and stronger.

May you find a connection to the holy in these poems. May you know yourself to also be holy.

Awakening

for Shay

Something ancient stirs in me
stretches long-unused limbs
tests a voice kept silent for too long
as I find myself drawn back
to ritual
to music sung by female voices
to goddesses
to priestesses
to images of the divine feminine
to solstices and equinoxes
      and sacred connection to the Earth who is our mother
to embodied prayer
      arms raised to the sky, a gesture of invocation
      rather than hands folded demurely in supplication
you are not the source of this
any more than I am
(though we both are vessels for it)
and yet you were the catalyst
you opened me to it again
after years of shutting it away
denying it
pretending it was only a fanciful part of my past
something I had outgrown
with fairy tales
and stories that ended with "happily ever after"
the power runs through my veins again
my spine straightens and I am taller
my roots go deep and I am grounded
I am powerful again
I am powerful
I am

Letter from Gaia

As all children
eventually leave
the homes of their parents,
so you have left me,
following a new way,
entering a new realm.

I do not mind that so much,
knowing it is part of your growth,
except that you seem to have
forgotten me,
relegated me
to the distant past.

Do you not see that I am still here?

I am
the green grass
beneath your feet,
when you remember
to walk barefoot
on the earth,
my body.

I am
the moon shining
in the night sky—
my light is,
I am,
more than a reflection
of the sun.

I am the mother
of the new young god
who is at the center
of the new home
you have made for yourself.

The separation
between him and me—
and thus between you and me—
is a false one of your making...
in the realm of spirit,
there is no cutting
of an umbilical cord
to sever mother from child.

I may be exiled from your new life,
my many images
may no longer be honored
as they once were,
but I am no less present
no less loving
than any mother
whose heart remains
always
with her children.

The Power

I stand tall
fists raised to the sky
and I call the storm
I call the lightning to me—
or do I send it
from within the depths
of my soul
to sear the heavens?

I call the thunder
and I scream with it
cursing the hatred
the pain
the death
chasing it all away

By the very power
of darkness
I come back
into the light.

She Who Sees

Something is wrong
somewhere
right now
someone, something
just died
just ceased
to exist
and it hurts
it is Pain
all-encompassing
blinding darkness
falling forever

I feel the death
I hear the sigh
of the final breath
I am She Who Sees
I am Priestess
I am Mother
Hear my cries.

Vespers

I read the words assigned to me
    the last third of an Imbolc poem
    by another woman writer

I'd read them before, a week ago,
    when our team chose the poem
    as the centerpiece of tonight's service
        but had forgotten,
           and agreed to read whatever part was needed.

Ah, but then…

I began to speak,
    and You settled yourself into me
        my vocal cords, as I spoke clearly and firmly
        my spine, as I straightened in my chair
           almost obeying an urge to stand
                to raise my arms above my head
                    in power and in invocation
    and through the poem's words
        spoken in my own voice
        You reminded me
           that I am Yours
           that I am You
           that I cannot be made smaller
                or less powerful
                without my consent
           that I must claim the truth
                of who I am
                    and damn the consequences.

    I cannot stay
        where my presence is contained
           trapped in a box called "Should"
        where I am not permitted
           to rise, to stand, to speak truth
                using words and gestures of power
                    both mine and that which flows through me
                    from a source older than any name
                      used to contain it

They call my power, my courage
    "a strong personality"
      in a tone that makes clear
        they find it too much,
          unseemly for a woman minister

They got more than they bargained for
    and now they have two choices:
      receive the gift gratefully
        or lose it as I leave.

They have underestimated me
    at every turn
      seeing the Maiden or the Mother
        not recognizing I am also Goddess
          and approaching Crone
        and I have no time for or interest in
          the small boxes they made for me.

International Women's Day

My social media feed
    was full of strong women all day
        the famous ones
        the fictional ones
        the mythological ones
        the archetypal ones
        and the ones I know
            in "real life"

Full, too, of messages I needed to see
    be your full self
        whether "they" like it or not
    claim your power
    tell your truth
    don't apologize for who you are

We ended the day with a woman superhero
    Captain Marvel

All day long
    just under the surface of my skin
        a faint tingle reminds me
            of the power I carry.

Lilith

I.

I recognize the pattern
slowly becoming less than whole
until you can't take it another day
          another breath

and a scream of rage
          shatters the illusion of
                    "I'm great, thanks"

          and declares an end
                    to the life you've been
                              inhabiting
                                        without fully living.

II.

Don't ask me
to contemplate Lilith today
and find myself in her story.

I'm too angry
to wield her power wisely.

I might just
toss a lit match
over my shoulder
as I walk away
with a grim smile
never looking back.

Holy Rage

I feel You
        pushing at the seams
                of my carefully-constructed
                        (not by me, at least not entirely)
                                ministerial politeness

I am ready to rage
        to turn over tables
                to tell people
                        when they are acting like toddlers
                        instead of
                                emotionally and spiritually
                                      mature adults
        to ground myself into Your power
                which is also my power
      to shine
                until they avert their eyes because
                    I am too bright for them.

Presence

"My daughter, I am always right here, and you are always okay."[1]

You hover nearby
> always present
>> whether I notice or not

>> grandmother, teacher, mother, goddess
>>> source of wisdom and compassion

> and when needed
>> fierce protection
>>> holy rage
>>>> pure power

It is your comfort
> I most often seek

but when under siege
> I welcome your
>> purifying fire.

[1] Source Unknown.

Return

In this time of stress
    I turn again to
        goddesses
        priestesses
        women of power and light
    their images
    their words
    their stories
    their Presence
        sustains me
        strengthens me
        emboldens me
        fills me

until I no longer know
    how it's possible
        that no one sees
            a physical change
                come over me

as I hold my ground
    unshaken by their petty behavior
    grounded with roots so deep
        they cannot move me

They do not know yet
    what they have begun

Altars

I.

Talking about our future home
      and altars in it
      you say
            "I hope our whole home
                will be about the feminine divine"

My soul leaps
      and I smile

knowing this, too,
      is part of our connection
            and why we are together.

II.

Make an altar
not just of a single shelf
or dresser-top

not even of a whole room
or a home filled with love
and celebration
of the divine feminine

but of my life
      my work
      my way of
           moving in the world.

May I be consecrated
      to the service of Love
           and her public face, Justice
      and to the Life
           that infuses
           and illuminates
           everything.

Birthing

Reading a novel
I come to a passage
     describing a birth
     from the mother's perspective

I remember, dimly
     the bodily sensations
     especially the urgency
          of the last push

and also the power
     something new in my body
          and my spirit
an awareness of my own divinity
     and the sacred power
          of giving life
          and giving birth
          to that new life

something primal, primeval
     connecting me to a lineage
          of mothers, stretching back
               into the mists before history

That was the day
I felt the full shift
from Maiden to Mother

Now that baby is a young man
and I am moving
from Mother to Wise Woman
          Elder?
          Crone?

Entering a new phase of life
no less powerful
(perhaps even more)
than when I bore him
     into the world

Beyond the Page

Delving into these tales
        set in Troy, Atlantis, Avalon

I enjoy them
        but don't devour them
                with the hunger I once felt
                the amazement at worlds
                populated by goddesses
                and priestesses

Now I sense a new craving
to move beyond
reading fiction filled with
        the divine feminine
into a spiritual life
        suffused with Her presence.

Solstice Sisters

Winter solstice
The longest night

I remember the years
of singing in ritual
with my "solstice sisters"

One year, we stayed all night
and sang to the rising sun.

This year, no singing for me
after two years of the ritual
with a different group
      all genders
      more inclusive,
           which I honor

Yet I crave goddess-song
      with those beloved women's voices
         rising together
            by candlelight.

Connection

I am ready
        to build a new altar
                to You
                        the Goddess
                        the divine feminine
                        Mother of Us All[2]
                        She Who Sees

Ready to surround myself
        with images of You
        with chants sung to You
                in female voices

to light candles
        to learn prayers
                to write poems

to connect with You
        within myself
        between me and my Beloved
        in all of life
                and love

---

[2] from Jennifer Berezan's song "Returning"

Section 3: Social Justice

"Justice is what Love looks like in public." -Cornel West

Section Introduction

Social justice, like love, has been a theme in my writing since my early days—perhaps not childhood, but certainly by my college years. On New Year's Day 1990, when I was 19 years old, I wrote this:

Our Time Now

This is our time—
we children of the Seventies
are grown now
in college, or working somewhere
living our lives

We are at the crossroads
child to adult
past to present
student to teacher

What will we do with these years,
the Nineties?
They are ours to live.
Let us live them well.
It is our time now.

We can change the world
if we're only willing to try
We can make a difference
if we can only take the time
We have the strength, the will
The courage is ours
We can build our world
It is our time now.

I kept writing about justice, including in poetry and in a monthly newspaper parenting column I wrote for most of the first ten years of my son's life. For a while, I hosted a website called Poetic Justice as a home for justice-related poetry by me and others.

Over time, as I answered the call to ministry, my justice work became centered in my work with and for congregations, though I continued to write occasional justice-focused blog posts. I often became restless, feeling like my words were not reaching an audience where they would make a difference.

At a clergy retreat in April 2018, I journaled:

> There is danger that I am "preaching to the choir"--what actual <u>change</u> in the world happens as a result? Am I moving us (Unitarian Universalists, a particular congregation, readers) to act as Love's agents more than we already were? What is the tangible outcome? Which topics/oppressions/people have I included and which have I left out?
>
> For example, I changed the Social Justice candle sung response, removing a hymn with binary gendered language, but the replacement hymn has a line about "all of us imprisoned" which touches a nerve for [a congregant whose son was imprisoned] and maybe others. My intent was to be more inclusive, and I hear that lyric as supporting those who are literally imprisoned, but the impact on [the congregant] matters.

This book, written not for a single congregation or members of a particular faith tradition, is a step on my journey to spreading a message of Justice as a form of Love to a wider audience. Thank you for joining me in that journey!

Herstory

(Or, Sandra Fluke Was Not The First)

Jewish Lilith
was called
whore
because she saw herself
as Adam's equal
in bed and elsewhere.

Her replacement, Eve,
was called
temptress
because she dared to offer
Adam a chance at knowledge
and took some for herself.

Trojan Kassandra
was called
crazy
because she tried to warn her people
of the coming destruction,
suggested that her brother's choice of bride
might have serious consequences.

Roman Diana
was called
man-hater
because she didn't believe
women should be subject to men,
didn't like Peeping Toms near her bath,
preferred to remain single.

British Morgaine
was called
witch
because she believed in
something older
than their new young god,
believed in Avalon
rather than Glastonbury.

The moral of these stories:
women,
write your own biographies.

Four Women Claim Their Voices

I.

You do not see me.
Maybe because I have
  allowed myself
  to become invisible
    camouflaged to disappear
    into my surroundings.
I take a deep breath
  stand tall, both feet
    firmly on the ground
  and allow myself to appear
  allow you to see me.
There is no return
  to invisibility
  once you
    stand in the light.

II.

I have turned sideways into the light
  and disappeared to you.
Accustomed to only seeing me
  in the way you want to,
  you think I am gone.
To those who knew me before
  I have reappeared
  stepping into the light
  fully present again
That other me, the one you wounded
  and then left
  is not dead.
  She was never real, only a
    projection of my fears
     and your anger.
This me,
  the woman of strength, of joy, of delight in the world
  is the me I want
  my son to know.

III.

I am not defined
      by your labels for me
   not limited
      by your perception of me
   not diminished
      by your rejection of me
I might stumble for a moment
         over roadblocks you place
            in my path
but the path is bigger than you
      and I will not be stopped.

IV

You think you see me
      think you know me.

You are wrong.

You see what I reveal
      know what I share
but that is only part of me.

You are misled
         distracted
      by labels and roles
         you think define me.

Happily Ever After

In the books and movies
      it's signaled with a kiss
      or lovers embracing.
We are raised on these stories
      almost from birth.
      Princesses and princes.
      Damsels and knights.
      Couples, always—
      and always
      one male, one female.
That leaves out so many
      kinds of love stories
      some of which have
            nothing to do
            with romance
            and everything to do
            with loving ourselves
            happily ever after

Kristallnacht

Tonight I went to a ceremony
        in remembrance of Kristallnacht,
        the beginning of the Holocaust.

My friend and I arrived late, and
        the candles which were handed out
        were already all taken.

We stood at the back of the crowd,
        willing to watch and listen
        without a candle.

A man turned to us,
        saw that we had no candles,
        and gave us his.

In doing so, he extended to us
        not only a flame to carry,
        but a bit of the love
        and unity
        that is so necessary
        if the horror of Kristallnacht
        is not to be repeated.

Our Mother's Keepers

This world is not ours
to destroy
to desecrate
to rape

If we must believe
that it belongs to someone
then let us believe
that it belongs
to our children
and that we are merely
its guardians
here to
protect
preserve
defend.

The Dove Points the Way

So many wars   because we see god
differently   (think ours is better,   we are chosen)

we lose sight of   each other and
the fact that   (if there is a god)
she or he or they   sees us   all the same
flawed, but   worthy of love

We even make war   on the earth
not realizing   we are factory-farming ourselves
genetically modifying god

The dove soars   sees us all
mourns itself

You say   "God is all"
I say   all is god
You say   "God remakes us"
I say   we remake god

The dove says   we are both right

We are looking at each other   through god
from opposite ends   of a rifle scope

The dove drops withered leaves   from the olive branch
a desperate trail for us   to follow

Privilege and Oppression

Federal workers in line for free food
transgender military members deemed "unfit"
racist white boys invited to the White House
and the usual backdrop of lies and crimes

This all feels so surreal
like it can't really be happening
       but I know that's my privilege speaking

The rich have never taken care of those with less
       ("missing a paycheck or two is no big deal")

Homophobia and transphobia are everywhere

Indigenous people and black and brown people
       have been victims of colonization and abuse
       since white people first came to this land

and power has always attracted the corrupt.

It's just not hidden from some of us
       (the ones who ever had the option
           of not seeing it)
           anymore.

Self-Care for Activists

When it seems like
      the whole world is on fire

Sometimes it is okay
      to focus on just your little corner
         and find what you can do

cook a meal for yourself
spend time with loved ones
read a novel that takes you away
      on a mental vacation
         until you can take a physical one
take a nap

Put on your own oxygen mask first.
You can't help others
      let alone save the world
if you are suffocating.

Holy Family

That phrase doesn't just mean Jesus, Mary, and Joseph.

My holy family is
  two women
  and a teenage boy

Holy families of brown-skinned children
  and their parents or other guardians
    arrive daily seeking refuge.

Holy families
  worship   in churches
        in synagogues
        in mosques
        in temples
        in nature

   sing and drum and chant
       in all the languages of
         the human, holy family

We Rise

"I don't have anything to prove to you." Carol Danvers/Captain Marvel

That's right.
I don't have to justify myself to you
       not my actions
              my words
              my appearance
              my existence

"I've been fighting with one arm behind my back. What will happen now that I'm free?"
Carol Danvers/Captain Marvel

Patriarchy tried to keep us restrained
       but we are rising
              breaking those bonds
                     showing our strength

Stand back.

You have underestimated us
       for far too long.

Today, we rise.

Grieving for Trees

These particular trees were removed
      not for profit
      but due to damage
      and risk of them falling
         on buildings or people

and yet, the stumps and debris
      the sight of truckloads of logs
         makes me sad

takes me back to a memory
      driving from Portland to the Oregon coast years ago
         and smelling sawdust
            confused by the scent
        until I rounded a corner
           and saw a clear-cut hillside
           freshly ravaged

I can still smell it today.

Peacemaker

I'm a peacemaker by nature
    a 9 on the Enneagram*
    a pacifist from a military family

I tend to be conflict avoidant
    but on some issues
        there is no middle ground
        there is a clear right and wrong
    and in those situations
        I will speak truth to power
            to family
            to friends
            to congregants
      to whoever will listen
    and I will not be silenced
        or agree to "meet in the middle"
        to make peace

"No justice, no peace"
    and we are far, so far
        from anything like justice

so don't expect me to be ladylike
        or even polite
    when the world is on fire
        and you stubbornly
           look away
                from the smoke
                and ash

*I later learned that I am actually a 1 with a very strong 9 wing.

How Often Society Punishes the Angry Woman

We are taught from birth
    to be good little girls
        use our manners
        and our inside voices

So when we stop being polite
    or let out a scream
        of pain or fury
    society is shocked
        repelled by our defiance
           of the rules
             we were
                steeped in.

We are ignored
    or labeled bitch
    or accused of having PMS
    or postpartum depression
    or menopause
    or some other "female trouble"

Our trouble is, we're angry
    and no one wants to listen.

"Take yourself seriously."

What would it mean to do that?
>What would I need to do, or stop doing?

Take care of the one body I get for this lifetime.
Take equally good care of my spirit.
Take up the space I inhabit,
>physically and energetically,
>without apology.

Take chances without fear
>of succeeding
>and making someone else uncomfortable.

Stop playing small
>or allowing others to diminish me

Own my power and channel it
>for the highest good

Be all of who I am, all the time
>no holds barred

Say yes to invitations that resonate,
>let go of anything that doesn't.

Worship.
Love.
Play.
Write.

Be the change.
Be the one I have been waiting for.

Women's Bodies

Chinese footbinding
      a delicate euphemism
      for intentional disabling

Victorian corsets and bustles
      an "ideal" figure
      no woman has naturally

Hobble skirts
      even the name admits
      the intent to limit mobility

Spike heels with pointy toes
      (notice the shape's similarity
      to footbinding)

Mandatory transvaginal ultrasound
      prior to abortion

The repeal of Roe v. Wade

Is it the myth of Creation,
      Eve formed from Adam's rib,
      that makes some men think
      they own our bodies,
      can control them?

Fourth of July

2019

The fireworks nearby
        sound like gunshots
Not a celebratory sound
        but a reminder of the violence
                woven into our nation's history
                        since its earliest days
                                (but not the earliest days
                                      of those who first called
                                          this land home)

I can't celebrate tonight
        not freedom from tyranny
                when a tyrant occupies
                        the Oval Office
        not "the land of the free"
                when children sleep in cages
        not "one nation indivisible"
                when the God added later
                        is used to justify divisions
                                and vilify people
        not "America the Beautiful"
                when we are killing the planet
                and desecrating
                the remaining wild places

Tomorrow there may be hope
        but tonight
                I am mourning.

2020

I can no longer enjoy
sparklers and fireworks
red, white, and blue clothing
the unthinking patriotism
        of my childhood

I can no longer observe
   "Independence Day"
any more than
   "Columbus Day"
or "Presidents Day"

all celebrations
of the "founding" of a nation
built on white supremacy,
the theft of land
and of people,
and oppressions
still alive and well today.

An Easier World

As I read today
        the "prequel" of Princess Leia
        at age sixteen (your age now)
I wondered how much you
        might feel like she did
        watching a tyrant take over bit by bit
        knowing she'd have to choose
                resistance
                or complicity

I wanted an easier world for you
        one we probably never really had
        (but those of us with privilege thought we did)
A world where you could believe
        in your government
        in the safety of your planet
        in a future without limits

I feel guilty sometimes
        for bringing you into <u>this</u> world
        but I honestly didn't know then

nor would I have chosen a life
        without the joy of you in it.

May I always do all I can
        to make the world safer for you
        and all parents' children.

96

Identities

"Poet and activist"
      I said with sudden clarity
      nearly fourteen years ago

"Minister" took over
      but I am reclaiming "poet"
      and will work to earn "activist"
            in this world
                  which needs all three.

Rising and Lifting

"We rise by lifting each other"
      my new t-shirt says

a message not just about
      the acrobatics of Cirque du Soleil

but also about
      the reality of life

      (despite all the human behavior
      designed to lift only some
      on the backs of others)

We rise
      by lifting each other

Amen.

A Visit to ICE

She was seven,
    shy,
      and bilingual.
Her mother spoke only Spanish
      and I, only English
      so a translator accompanied us
      to the meeting with US Immigration and Customs Enforcement.

I drove the seventy miles
      from their home in Greeley
      to the Denver Field Office

She was silent in the backseat
      except, as we got closer,
      to tell the translator
      that her tummy hurt.

Of course it did.

On a previous visit
      her mother was detained for months;
      she was taken in by kind neighbors
      until her mother's eventual release.

She held my hand as we walked in.

I made a rookie mistake,
      had something in my purse
      that violated the rules
but my white skin
      and my clerical collar
         bought me some grace
    so I was sent to leave it in my car
      and then passed through
         the metal detector successfully.
This time, her mother
      came out of the appointment
      with instructions to return
         in one year.

A year of grace.
A year of lessened worry for them both.

On the car ride home
      she talked nearly nonstop,
      giving me my first
      Spanish lesson,
      giggling at words I didn't know.

Echoes

Indefinite detention of immigrants
      including children

Detention centers with no outside monitoring
      ICE answerable only to themselves

A leader talking about staying in office
      beyond the legal term limit

Claims that Jewish Americans
      aren't fully loyal to this nation

eerie echoes of eighty years ago.

Deportations, August 2019*

Deportations
are often death sentences
  people sent back to violence
  or persecution
  or starvation

but this is so blatant
  33 days
  get out
  no more medical treatment

It's not a death sentence
  it's murder

  and our president
    is the murderer.

The blood is on the hands
  of every MAGA hat-wearing
  "build the wall"-screaming
  Trump supporter

but also on the hands of
  everyone who voted for him
    (or will next year)
  and every Senator or Congressional Representative
    not calling for
      immediate impeachment.

News broke in that month that changes to immigration policy by the Trump administration meant that hundreds of immigrant children receiving life-saving medical care in the United States faced deportation.

September 11th

2008

September 11th again.

The only news I watch today
will be the Lehrer News Hour on PBS.
I feel reasonably sure that they, at least,
will not spin today's seventh anniversary
for political gain or to raise viewership
by appealing to our voyeuristic tendency
to want to watch others' tragedies
over and over and over.

The only radio station I will listen to today is NPR.
The commercial stations
always turn this day into a
"patriotic" memorial
full of bluster
about how great we are
and how awful "they" are.

Even NPR's coverage,
which is both short and fairly objective,
leaves me with tears on my face
cradling the pain of that day
to me
like a fragile egg
resting in the pit of my stomach.

As I eat my lunch in front of the computer,
I reread my little brother's
latest email from Iraq,
subject line "Alive and Well,"
announcing his arrival there
for his third deployment
(four if you count Afghanistan too)
in seven years.

Don't anyone wave a flag at me
or tell me "never forget."

More than two towers crashed down on that day.

2019

Writing that date
always takes me back

Waking up in Georgia
to a phone call from a friend in Connecticut
"Turn on the news."

I did, in time to see
the second tower hit
then to learn about the Pentagon
and Flight 93's passengers
forcing a rural crash
instead of a fourth target
(where were they aiming?)

I watched in horror
as the towers fell

people running away
through the dust clouds
(first responders
still running to the site)

people jumping
(did we see that live on air
or do I only remember
the iconic photos later?)

My only child was born
not quite 14 months later.

He has never lived
in a pre-9/11 America
(or in an America not at war
ever since that attack
justified the War on Terror)
an America without the PATRIOT Act and ICE.

The anniversaries
are all too often used
to stoke nationalism
America the heroic victim
Islam the religion of violence
(neither is accurate)

I mourn what was lost that day
not only the lives
of all those who never showed up
at the waiting emergency rooms

but the era of relative peace
my own childhood
lived largely between
the war in Viet Nam
and Desert Storm.

"Never forget"
is more complex
than many want to admit.

2020

Nineteen years ago
the towers fell
and our world changed

This year
        exponentially more people dead
        exponentially more change
                in ways that impact us all
                    every single day

Why do we as a nation mourn
        that smaller loss
while downplaying this
        enormous one?

Perhaps because then
        we could blame "the evildoers"

and now the real evildoers
        are running the government.

Election Year (2020)

Hope begins to bloom
     hope that we can win the election
     hope that we can oust the fascist
     hope that we can repair
          not only what he has broken
          but the underlying,
               centuries-old brokenness
               starkly revealed in these years
               to those of us who had
               enough privilege
               to avoid seeing it before.

I tenderly nourish the hope
     while also admitting to fear
     because I no longer trust
     that anyone playing fair
     can still win here.

Strong Women Characters

I steep myself
        in story after story
                of strong women
                spiritual women
                warriors for good

Morgaine
Paksennarion[3]
Leia

Feeling my way
        toward what they found
                what they represent

        what lives within me

        the power of a woman
                who knows herself
                and answers a call
                        larger than herself

[3] source: Elizabeth Moon's "The Deed of Paksennarion" trilogy

Suffering or Freedom

A new tool tonight
  a question
    "Does this contribute
      to my suffering
        or to my freedom?"

My immediate response:
  "There's the answer to my sabbatical dilemma."

but I also think of
  all the times in the past
    when I could have used that
      might have turned toward freedom
       sooner
       with more confidence
       with less fear
      might have prevented (or reduced)
       my own suffering
         and that of people I love

A second layer is needed:
  a recognition
    that ethical use of my privilege
      may sometimes mean
        choosing another's freedom

Faith in the Future

I want my son
        to have faith in the future
        but worry that would be
                misleading him

Climate collapse
        and rising nationalism
                and fascism
        make me fear for the future
                in my own lifetime
                        let alone his

We have failed
        to leave our children
                a world at least as good
                        as the one we were born into

Where is the political will
        to change course
                before it's too late?

I fear we may already
        have passed the point
                of no return

What can I say to my son
        except I love you
                and I'm sorry?

The Secret

The secret, he says,
      is simple—
         three little words:
         "I love you."

He speaks of lies
      told to us
         by our government

And asks us
      how we can
         accept being deceived.

After hearing Mike Farrell speak on "International Human Rights" at the Nebraska Model United Nations Keynote Address at the University of Nebraska on February 27, 1991.

Minimalism

I.

naming racism
wherever I witness it
the least I can do

II.

how ridiculous
that I fear backlash when I
write the simple truth

Queer Marriage in the Era of the Trump Supreme Court Appointees

I don't want our legal marriage
to be about protection
from a tyrannical government
which threatens
our civil rights.

I want it to be about
our deep love for each other
and our commitment to that love
and our desire to be together
for the rest of our lives.

We both used to say
our pasts made us leery
of "forever"
and I want any marriage vows
to be reflective of a change
in that belief,
not a change in national politics.

I want to propose to you
not as a practical matter
but as a passionate one,
from the depth of my love
rather than our fear.

and yet...
the fear is real
and, sadly, probably realistic.

How, then, do we proceed?

I resent our current culture
for yet again
making couples like us
face decisions like these.

Numb Haiku (February 5, 2020)

it's a grumpy day
no true disasters, and yet
little crap adds up

one big disaster
the Senate acquitted Trump
democracy died

no wonder I'm numb
and so I am just grumpy
instead of keening

Cut it Out

Cut out the words that hurt you
> that diminished you
> that belittled you
> that cut you

the pages on which
> you did not appear
>> were invisible
>> were lied about
>> were caricatured

the books in which
> you couldn't find home
>> or an anchor
>> or anyone from your world

all the language which denied you
> oppressed you
> enslaved you

Cut it all out
> and from the tattered remains
> and the spaces freshly opened
>> create your own
>>> insert your I
>>>> into the narrative.

Afterword

Whether you read this book from front to back, or skipped around in it, I hope you have experienced a journey through three aspects of Love: loving yourself, including your body; love for the divine, in a way that reflects your own divinity back to you; and love for the world, expressed through a desire to call for (and work for) justice for all.

My own journey was inspired by many people, books, songs, movies, and more. I want to lift up just a handful of favorites in case you'd like to follow me down the rabbit hole!

Our society makes it hard for most of us to love our bodies—especially those of us who are marginalized due to gender, sexual orientation, disability, age, race, or other factors that make us not fit into the "ideal" promoted by so much of our culture. There are increasing numbers of books and other resources for those of us on the journey to reclaim (or claim for the first time) a sense of our bodies as sacred. I especially commend to you Sonya Renee Taylor's The Body Is Not an Apology: The Power of Radical Self-Love.

One of the ways those of us who are women (whether cisgender or transgender) are marginalized is by the dominance of words and images of the holy depicted as male. Claiming ourselves as divine in our own right, and also in the image of a divinity that is feminine, is a step to challenging patriarchal forms of spirituality. In this realm, again, there are many great resources. For a historical approach, I recommend Riane Eisler's powerful The Chalice and the Blade: Our History, Our Future. For a personal narrative of discovering the divine feminine, I suggest Sue Monk Kidd's Dance of the Dissident Daughter: A Woman's Journey from Christian Tradition to the Sacred Feminine. There are also a growing number of writers imagining the divine as nonbinary or genderqueer. As a cisgender woman, I hesitate to name a favorite, but am glad to see the expansion of how we all imagine the divine.

Social justice as an expression of love is crucial to our future, and the future of our planet. The more we can center the voices of those who have been marginalized, the faster and deeper this work will be. I've said it in the introduction but want to say again how grateful I am to Tehom Center Publishing for making this their explicit mission. If you feel called to add your voice to the chorus, I encourage you to check out www.tehomcenter.org.

If you'd like to connect with me, you can find me at www.sacreddepths.com, where my wife, the Rev. Shay MacKay, and I offer an entrepreneurial ministry with the mission of connecting people with the sacred (as each person understands and experiences it) through creativity and contemplation.

When you participate in an offering through Sacred Depths, whether a workshop, retreat, or spiritual direction, you will be given time, space, and resources to connect more deeply with the divine within and beyond yourself. Participants frequently tell us that these experiences have been life-changing for them, as they move into a deeper relationship with themselves, other people, and the holy. For some, it is the first time that they encounter the idea that they have an inner wisdom, and that they are themselves whole and holy, no matter the circumstances of their lives. We believe that by offering these opportunities to individuals, we change not only their lives, but the lives of their families, their communities, and thus the world.

We invite *you* to join us in making Love real in the world.

Printed in the USA
CPSIA information can be obtained
at www.ICGtesting.com
CBHW051739150824
13134CB00044B/828